Peer Gessing

PERFECTION FOR YOU

Peer Gessing

PERFECTION FOR YOU

Impressum

Bibliografische Information der Deutschen Nationalbibliothek

Die Deutsche Nationalbibliothek verzeichnet diese Publikation in der Deutschen Nationalbibliografie; detaillierte bibliografische Daten sind im Internet über http://dnb.d-nb.de abrufbar.

TWENTYSIX-Der Self-Publishing-Verlag
Eine Kooperation zwischen der Verlagsgruppe
Random House und BoD-Books on Demand

© 2017 Peer Gessing

Herstellung und Verlag:
BoD – Books on Demand, Norderstedt

ISBN 9 783740 729622

Table of Contents

Prolog

0

1 2 3 4 5 6 7 8 9 10

11 12 13 14 15 16 17 18 19 20

21 22 23 24 25 26 27 28 29 30

31 32 33 34 35 36 37 38 39 40

41 42 43 44 45 46 47 48 49 50

51 52 53 54 55 56 57 58 59 60

61 62 63 64 65 66 67 68 69 70

71 72 73 74 75 76 77 78 79 80

81 82 83 84 85 86 87 88 89 90

91 92 93 94 95 96 97 98 99 100

start your creativity

Perfection

starts in your heart
and will be a part of the eternity.

zero

one

2

two

3

three

four

5

five

6

six

seven

8

eight

9

nine

01

10

ten

11

eleven

12

twelve

13

thirteen

14

fourteen

15

fiveteen

16

16

sixteen

17

seventeen

eighteen

18

eighteen

19

nineteen

20

20

twenty

21

twenty-one

22

twenty-two

23

twenty-three

24

twenty-four

25

twenty-five

26

Twenty-six

26

twenty-six

27

twenty-seven

82

28

twenty-eight

29

twenty-nine

30

30

thirty

31

thirty-one

32

32

thirty-two

33

thirty-three

34

thirty-four

35

thirty-five

36

36

thirty-six

37

thirty-seven

38

thirty-eight

39

thirty-nine

04

40

fourty

41

fourty-one

42

42

fourty-two

43

fourty-three

44

fourty-four

45

fourty-five

46

fourty-six

47

fourty-seven

48

fourty-eight

49

fourty-nine

50

fifty

51

fifty-one

52

fifty-two

53

fifty-three

54

fifty-four

55

fifty-five

56

fifty-six

57

fifty-seven

58

fifty-eight

59

fifty-nine

08

60

sixty

61

sixty-one

62

sixty-two

63

sixty-three

64

sixty-four

65

sixty-five

66

sixty-six

67

sixty-seven

80

68

sixty-eight

69

sixty-nine

70

seventy

71

seventy-one

72

seventy-two

73

seventy-three

74

seventy-four

75

seventy-five

76

seventy-six

77

seventy-seven

78

seventy-eight

79

seventy-nine

03

80

eighty

81

eighty-one

28

82

eighty-two

83

eighty-three

N° 8

84

eighty-four

85

eighty-five

86

eighty-six

87

eighty-seven

88

88

eighty-eight

89

eighty-nine

90

ninety

91

ninety-one

26

92

ninety-two

93

ninety-three

94

ninety-four

95

ninety-five

96

ninety-six

97

ninety-seven

89

98

ninety-eight

99

ninety-nine

100

one hundred

Perfection for you

The blank pages are waiting for completion through your personal drawings, texts, poems, findings or memories.

$1 + 2 + 3 + 4 = 10$, this is a triangle by Pythagoras and at the same time the blueprint for a pyramid.
We must be ready every day to build a new world.

One hundred pages.
One hundred years.
One hundred days.

...